SUPER SANDCASTLE
State Stories

# LEAPING LILY

## ~ A Story About Georgia ~

Written by Colleen Dolphin

Illustrated by Bob Doucet

Consulting Editor, Diane Craig, M.A./Reading Specialist

**ABDO**
Publishing Company

Published by ABDO Publishing Company
8000 West 78th Street, Edina, Minnesota 55439.

Printed in the United States of America, North Mankato, Minnesota
112009
012010

 PRINTED ON RECYCLED PAPER

Editor: Katherine Hengel
Content Developer: Nancy Tuminelly
Cover and Interior Design: Anders Hanson, Mighty Media
Production: Colleen Dolphin, Mighty Media
Photo Credits: iStockphoto (Doug Allen, Thomas Harris,
Mark Strozier, David Sucsy), One Mile Up, SeaPics.com
(Larry Mishkar), Shutterstock, Stacie Wells, Leah Yetter.
Quarter-dollar coin image from the United States Mint.

**Library of Congress Cataloging-in-Publication Data**

Dolphin, Colleen, 1979-
  Leaping Lily : a story about Georgia / Colleen Dolphin ;
illustrated by Bob Doucet.
    p. cm. -- (Fact & fable: state stories)
  ISBN 978-1-60453-924-0
  1. Georgia--Juvenile literature.  I. Doucet, Bob, ill. II. Title.

  F286.3.D65 2010
  975.8--dc22
                        2009033464

Super SandCastle™ books are created by a team of professional
educators, reading specialists, and content developers around
five essential components—phonemic awareness, phonics,
vocabulary, text comprehension, and fluency—to assist young
readers as they develop reading skills and strategies and
increase their general knowledge. All books are written,
reviewed, and leveled for guided reading, early reading
intervention, and Accelerated Reader® programs for use in
shared, guided, and independent reading and writing activities
to support a balanced approach to literacy instruction.

# TABLE OF CONTENTS

Etowah
Indian Mounds
(pg. 17)

honeybee
(pg. 9)

green tree frog
(pg. 4)

Appalachian Trail
(pg. 19)

Cherokee roses
(pg. 16)

Athens

Atlanta

Douglasville

Chatahoochee River

GEORGIA

Augusta

brown thrasher
(pg. 10)

Macon

Columbus

Vidalia

Savannah
(pg. 8)

Georgia
Music Hall
of Fame
(pg. 12)

Albany

largemouth bass
(pg. 7)

Valdosta

right whale
(pg. 5)

LEGEND

★ CAPITAL

〜 RIVER

○ CITY

● STORY START

- - - STORY PATH

✦ STORY END

3

# LEAPING LILY

It was late fall on Jekyll Island near the coast of Georgia. Lily, a little green tree frog, was leaping along the beach. Suddenly, a huge whale burst from the ocean. Lily jumped back in surprise. "Maurice!" she cried. "You're home from your trip! How was it?"

"What an adventure!" Maurice exclaimed. "I saw so many new things."

"I'm going on an adventure myself," Lily said. "I'm heading north to hike the Appalachian Trail. I just need to find it."

"My friend Bobby can give you directions," said Maurice. "He's a largemouth bass. He lives in the Okefenokee Swamp."

"Great!" said Lily. "Thanks for the help."

"Good luck! See you when you get back!" said Maurice.

## Right Whale

The right whale is Georgia's state **marine mammal**. A right whale can be more than 50 feet (15 m) long! Instead of teeth, these whales have **baleen plates**. The baleen plates look like a comb across the whale's mouth.

## Okefenokee Swamp

The Okefenokee Swamp is the largest swamp in North America. The ground is mostly covered by peat. Peat is soft ground made of rotting plants. In some places, the trees shake when you stomp next to them. *Okefenokee* is a Native American word that means "land of the trembling earth."

A few days later, Lily arrived at the Okefenokee Swamp. She leapt onto a floating log to rest. How would she ever find Bobby? Lily looked down into the water and saw a group of bass swimming together. Lily put her head under the water and **gurgled**, "Bobby?"

One of the largemouth bass swam over to her. "Yes, that's me!"

"Wonderful!" exclaimed Lily. "Maurice sent me to find you. Can you tell me how to get to the Appalachian Trail?"

"Sure. Just go to Springer Mountain. That's where the trail starts. My friend Holly has been there. Maybe she could take you," Bobby said.

"Where can I find Holly?" Lily asked.

"Holly is a honeybee who lives in Savannah. You can find her buzzing around the fountain in Forsyth Park."

## Largemouth Bass

Georgia's state fish is the largemouth bass. It eats other fish, crawfish, and insects. It can also eat small birds and **mammals**. The largemouth bass has excellent senses. It can see, hear, and smell very well.

7

After days of leaping, Lily finally made it to Savannah. "What a beautiful city!" thought Lily. In Forsyth Park, she saw a fountain surrounded by colorful flowers. There were honeybees everywhere! Lily started looking for Holly.

"Holly?" called Lily. "Are any of you Holly?"

## Savannah

The city of Savannah was founded in 1733. Forsyth Park was the city's first public park. It is famous for its fancy iron fountain. The fountain was made to look like a fountain in Paris, France.

8

"I am!" said a little honeybee. She flew towards Lily. "How can I help you?"

"I'm so glad I found you!" said Lily. "I'm trying to find Springer Mountain and the Appalachian Trail. Your friend Bobby said you know the way. Could you take me there?"

"Why, sure!" said Holly. "I love visiting Springer Mountain. Let's go!"

## Honeybee

The state insect of Georgia is the honeybee. Each honeybee hive has one queen bee. Thousands of worker bees also live in the hive. Worker bees collect nectar from flowers to make honey. Some bees fly more than 6 miles (10 km) to find nectar.

9

On the way, Holly and Lily stopped in Macon. They found a shady spot in a peach tree.

"These peaches are delicious!" said Lily.

Suddenly a brown bird flew down and landed right in front of them. "Hi, I'm Dottie," said the bird.

## Brown Thrasher

The brown thrasher is the state bird of Georgia. It is found throughout the state. It has a long tail and yellow eyes. Brown thrashers can sing up to 3,000 different songs.

"I'm Lily, and this is Holly," said Lily. "We're on our way to the Appalachian Trail. We stopped here to take a break."

"Are you thirsty?" asked Dottie.

"We sure are!" said Lily and Holly.

"Follow me," said Dottie. She led them to a table and served them Southern sweet iced tea.

"This hits the spot!" said Lily.

## Southern Sweet Iced Tea

3 family-size tea bags

8 cups water

1 cup sugar

Put 2 cups of cold water in a pot. Add 3 family-size tea bags. Bring to a boil. Immediately remove the pot from the heat. Let the tea bags steep for about 10 minutes. Remove the tea bags. Pour the warm tea into a pitcher. Add sugar. Stir until the sugar is completely dissolved. Add 6 cups of cold water. Serve over ice.

## Peach

The peach is the Georgia state fruit. The peach originally came from China. The Chinese believed peaches brought good luck. More than 40 kinds of peaches are grown in Georgia. Georgia's nickname is the Peach State.

11

"I'm going to a **concert** at the Georgia Music Hall of Fame tonight," said Dottie. "Do you two want to come?"

"You bet, we love music!" said Lily.

## Georgia Music Hall of Fame

The Georgia Music Hall of Fame honors musicians from Georgia. Tune Town is its main **exhibit** hall. It is built to look like a small Georgia town. Each building features a different kind of music.

12

When they arrived, there were people everywhere! The musicians were setting up outside. "I see my friend Otis," said Dottie. "He is saving seats for us."

Dottie introduced them to Otis the southern flying squirrel. He was sitting in a live oak tree. "What a great view!" said Lily. The **concert** began, and they all danced to the music.

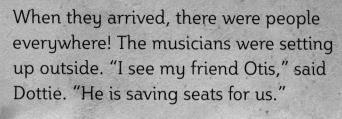

## Live Oak

The live oak is the state tree of Georgia. It has green leaves year round! Its branches can spread out more than 100 feet (30 m).

## Atlanta

Atlanta is the capital of Georgia. It is also the largest city in the state. There are many large companies in Atlanta such as Coca-Cola and Delta Air Lines.

The next day, Lily and Holly headed north to Atlanta. They went downtown to see what was there.

"Look, an aquarium!" said Lily.

"Let's check it out," said Holly.

Lily and Holly went right to the ocean **exhibit**. They saw many kinds of fish and sharks. They watched for a long time. "Are all of those creatures really in the ocean?" Lily asked.

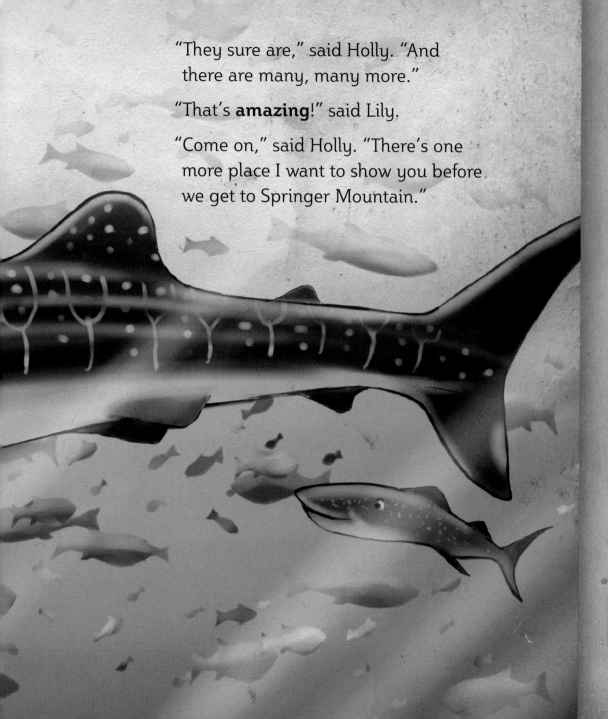

"They sure are," said Holly. "And there are many, many more."

"That's **amazing**!" said Lily.

"Come on," said Holly. "There's one more place I want to show you before we get to Springer Mountain."

## Georgia Aquarium

The Georgia Aquarium is the largest aquarium in the world! It has more than 8 million gallons of water. There are about 500 different **species** in the aquarium. Whale sharks, a giant squid, and a manta ray are a few examples.

## Cherokee Rose

The Cherokee rose is the Georgia state flower. It is a large, white flower with a yellow center. The flowers grow on a climbing **shrub** with thorny branches. It is also known as the camellia rose.

On the way, Lily spotted some beautiful white flowers growing on a bush. "Cherokee roses!" she said.

"Be careful!" said Holly. "The stems have thorns!"

"I'm just going to smell them," said Lily. "Ouch!"

Holly laughed and said, "Let's keep going!"

A little while later, they came to a hill. Lily thought maybe they were there. "Is this Springer Mountain?" she asked.

"No, these are the Etowah Indian Mounds. Native Americans lived here more than 500 years ago," explained Holly. They climbed a hill that was flat on top. They looked out over fields, trees, and the Etowah River.

"Thank you for bringing me here. I am so glad I saw this place," Lily told Holly.

## Etowah Indian Mounds

The Etowah Indian Mounds used to be a Native American village. Thousands of people lived there about 500 years ago. Since then, dirt has covered the village and created the mounds. **Archaeologists** study the mounds to learn about the people who lived there.

It was the last day of their journey. Holly and Lily could see the Blue Ridge Mountains up ahead. "We're almost there!" said Lily.

"You're going to have a fun trip," said Holly. "There is so much to see on the Appalachian Trail. There is no place like it!" As they approached Springer Mountain, Lily smiled and leapt with delight.

## Blue Ridge Mountains

The Blue Ridge Mountains are part of the Appalachian Mountains. From a distance, the mountains look blue! The Blue Ridge Mountains go from Pennsylvania to Georgia.

"Here we are," said Holly.

"Thank you so much," Lily said. "I've had such a great time!"

"You're welcome," said Holly. "Visit me again sometime!"

"I will! And I'll tell you all about my trip!" Then Lily waved to Holly and started leaping down the trail. Her Appalachian adventure was finally beginning!

# THE END

## Appalachian Trail

The Appalachian Trail is a path through the Appalachian Mountains. It is 2,175 miles (3,500 km) long and goes through 14 states. The south end is Springer Mountain in Georgia. The north end is Mount Katahdin in Maine. It can take five to seven months to walk the entire trail.

# Georgia at a Glance

**Abbreviation:** GA

**Capital:** Atlanta

**Largest city:** Atlanta (10th-largest U.S. city)

**Statehood:** January 2, 1788 (4th state)

**Area:** 59,441 square miles (153,952 sq km) (24th-largest state)

**Nickname:** Peach State

**Motto:** Wisdom, Justice, and Moderation

**State amphibian:** green tree frog

**State bird:** brown thrasher

**State fish:** largemouth bass

**State flower:** Cherokee rose

**State tree:** live oak

**State marine mammal:** right whale

**State insect:** honeybee

**State song:** "Georgia on My Mind"

**STATE SEAL**

**STATE FLAG**

**STATE QUARTER**

The Georgia quarter shows a peach in the center of the state outline. Live oak branches on either side are connected by a banner with the state motto, "Wisdom, Justice, and Moderation."

# WHAT DO YOU KNOW?

How well do you remember the story? Match the pictures to the questions below! Then check your answers at the bottom of the page!

**a.** Bobby

**b.** Cherokee rose

**c.** Appalachian Trail

**d.** Georgia Aquarium

**e.** Holly

**f.** peaches

1. What does Lily want to hike?

2. Who lives in Okefenokee Swamp?

3. Who does Lily meet in Forsyth Park?

4. What does Lily eat while resting in Macon?

5. Where does Lily see sharks?

6. What does Lily stop to smell on the way to Springer Mountain?

# What to Do in Georgia

**1** TAKE A HIKE
Tallulah Gorge State Park, Tallulah Falls

**2** SHOOT THE HOOCH
Chattahoochee River, Roswell

**3** EXPLORE A NATURE PRESERVE
Callaway Gardens, Pine Mountain

**4** WITNESS WILDLIFE
Bear Hollow Wildlife Trail, Athens

**5** STROLL DOWN A RIVERWALK
Augusta

**6** LEARN ABOUT U.S. HISTORY
Chickamauga & Chattanooga National Military Park

**7** LOOK OUT FROM A LIGHTHOUSE
Tybee Island Light Station, Tybee Island

**8** SEE GEORGIA'S "LITTLE GRAND CANYON"
Providence Canyon State Park, Lumpkin

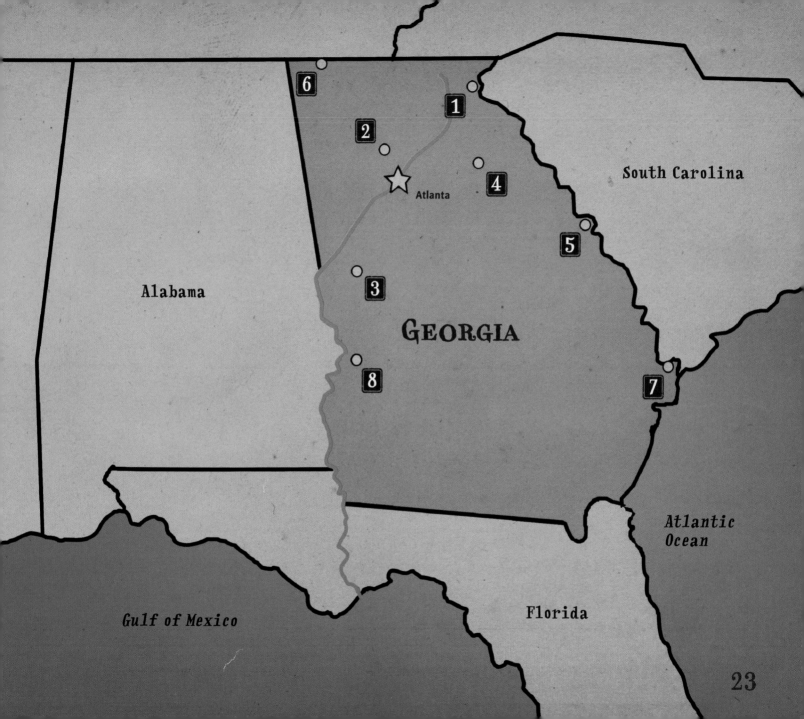

South Carolina

6

1

2

Atlanta

4

Alabama

5

3

GEORGIA

8

7

Atlantic
Ocean

Gulf of Mexico

Florida

23

# GLOSSARY

**amazing** – wonderful or surprising.

**archaeologist** – one who studies the remains of people and activities from ancient times.

**baleen plate** – one of the tooth-like plates that hangs from the upper jaw of baleen whales. These plates filter food from water.

**concert** – a musical performance.

**exhibit** – a display in a museum or aquarium.

**gurgle** – to speak with a bubbling sound.

**mammal** – a warm-blooded animal that has hair and whose females produce milk to feed their young.

**marine** – having to do with the sea.

**nocturnal** – most active at night.

**shrub** – a short plant with woody stems.

**species** – a group of related living beings.

**wetland** – a low, wet area of land such as a swamp or a marsh.

## About SUPER SANDCASTLE™

### Bigger Books for Emerging Readers
### Grades K–4

Created for library, classroom, and at-home use, Super SandCastle™ books support and engage young readers as they develop and build literacy skills and will increase their general knowledge about the world around them. Super SandCastle™ books are part of SandCastle™, the leading PreK–3 imprint for emerging and beginning readers. Super SandCastle™ features a larger trim size for more reading fun.

## Let Us Know

Super SandCastle™ would like to hear your stories about reading this book. What was your favorite page? Was there something hard that you needed help with? Share the ups and downs of learning to read. We want to hear from you! Send us an e-mail.

**sandcastle@abdopublishing.com**

Contact us for a complete list of SandCastle™, Super SandCastle™, and other nonfiction and fiction titles from ABDO Publishing Company.

www.abdopublishing.com • 8000 West 78th Street
Edina, MN 55439 • 800-800-1312 • 952-831-1632 fax